Dan Jinks   Bruce Cohen   Stage Entertainment USA
Roy Furman   Edward Walson   James L. Nederlander
Broadway Across America/Rich Entertainment Group   John Domo

IN ASSOCIATION WITH

Parrothead Productions   Lucky Fish   Peter May/Jim Fantaci   Harvey Weinstein/Carole L. Haber
Dancing Elephant Productions   CJ E&M   Ted Liebowitz   Ted Hartley   Clay Floren   Columbia Pictures

PRESENT

BigFish

BOOK BY
John August

MUSIC & LYRICS BY
Andrew Lippa

Based on the novel *Big Fish* by Daniel Wallace
and the Columbia Pictures film screenplay by John August

STARRING

Norbert Leo Butz   Kate Baldwin   Bobby Steggert

AND

Krystal Joy Brown   Anthony Pierini   Zachary Unger
Ryan Andes   Ben Crawford   Brad Oscar

WITH

JC Montgomery   Ciara Renée   Kirsten Scott   Sarrah Strimel

Preston Truman Boyd   Bree Branker   Alex Brightman   Joshua Buscher
Robin Campbell   Bryn Dowling   Jason Lee Garrett   Leah Hofmann   Synthia Link
Angie Schworer   Lara Seibert   Tally Sessions   Cary Tedder   Ashley Yeater

SCENIC DESIGN	COSTUME DESIGN	LIGHTING DESIGN	SOUND DESIGN
Julian Crouch	William Ivey Long	Donald Holder	Jon Weston

PROJECTION DESIGN	WIG & HAIR DESIGN	MAKE-UP DESIGN	CASTING
Benjamin Pearcy for 59 Productions	Paul Huntley	Angelina Avallone	Tara Rubin Casting

DANCE MUSIC ARRANGEMENTS	MUSIC COORDINATOR	VOCAL ARRANGEMENTS & INCIDENTAL MUSIC
Sam Davis	Michael Keller	Andrew Lippa

ADVERTISING & INTERACTIVE MARKETING	PRESS REPRESENTATIVE	ASSOCIATE DIRECTOR	ASSOCIATE CHOREOGRAPHER
SpotCo	The Hartman Group	Jeff Whiting	Chris Peterson

PRODUCTION MANAGEMENT	PRODUCTION SUPERVISOR	COMPANY MANAGER	GENERAL MANAGER
Aurora Productions	Joshua Halperin	David van Zyll de Jong	101 Productions, Ltd.

ORCHESTRATIONS
Larry Hochman

MUSIC DIRECTION
Mary-Mitchell Campbell

DIRECTION & CHOREOGRAPHY BY
Susan Stroman

Cover art: SpotCo

ISBN 978-1-4803-8365-4

HAL•LEONARD®
CORPORATION

7777 W. BLUEMOUND RD. P.O. BOX 13819 MILWAUKEE, WI 53213

In Australia Contact:
Hal Leonard Australia Pty. Ltd.
4 Lentara Court
Cheltenham, Victoria, 3192 Australia
Email: ausadmin@halleonard.com.au

Visit Hal Leonard Online at
www.halleonard.com

Andrew Lippa was commissioned to write the words and music to the original theatrical oratorio *I AM HARVEY MILK* that received its world premiere in San Francisco in June, 2013 with the San Francisco Gay Mens' Chorus starring Laura Benanti and Mr. Lippa as Harvey Milk. He also wrote the Tony-nominated music and lyrics to the hit Broadway musical *The Addams Family* with a book by Marshall Brickman and Rick Elice (*Jersey Boys*). Mr. Lippa wrote the music for the 2008 Broadway production of Aaron Sorkin's play *The Farnsworth Invention* directed by Des McAnuff. *The Wild Party* (book/music/lyrics) had its world premiere in 2000 at the Manhattan Theater Club in New York City. *The Wild Party* won the 1999-2000 Outer Critics Circle Award for Outstanding Off-Broadway Musical and Mr. Lippa won the 2000 Drama Desk Award for Outstanding Music. *Asphalt Beach* (music and lyrics) was premiered at Northwestern University by the American Music Theatre Project in October, 2006. 2004 saw the premiere of *A Little Princess* (book and lyrics by Brian Crawley) at Theatreworks in Palo Alto, CA. In 1999 he contributed three new songs to the Broadway version of *You're a Good Man, Charlie Brown* (including "My New Philosophy" for Tony® Award winner Kristin Chenoweth) and created all new arrangements. He wrote the music and co-wrote the book (with Tom Greenwald) for *john & jen*, which premiered in New York City in 1995 at The Lamb's Theater. He is currently working on a musical adaptation of Jules Feiffer's book *The Man in the Ceiling* and will be, for the first time, creating a role for himself in a new, full-length musical.

Mr. Lippa served as music director for Kristin Chenoweth for many of her prominent concerts. He conducted/played her sold-out shows at the Metropolitan Opera House in NYC in 2007, at Carnegie Hall in 2004, and at the Donmar Warehouse in London in 2002. He has conducted the San Francisco, Chicago, and St. Louis Symphony Orchestras for Ms. Chenoweth, among others.

Recordings include Julia Murney's CD *I'm Not Waiting* (producer, 3 songs), *I Am Harvey Milk* (produced by recording legend Leslie Ann Jones), *The Wild Party* (producer), *You're A Good Man, Charlie Brown* (producer) which earned him a GRAMMY® Award nomination, *The Addams Family* (producer), *A Little Princess* (producer), and *john & jen* (co-producer). Jazz phenom Peter Cincotti recorded the song "Raise the Roof" on his CD titled *On The Moon* (Phil Ramone, producer) Idina Menzel recently released "Life of the Party" on her *Barefoot at the Orchestra* CD and DVD (Marvin Hamlisch, conductor). In addition, Mr. Lippa produced the original cast recording of *Bat Boy* for RCA Victor and his singing voice can be heard on *The Sondheim Album* (on Fynsworth Alley) and *If I Sing* (on PS Classics.) Vocal selections and choral arrangements from *Big Fish*, *The Wild Party*, *The Addams Family*, and *john & jen* are published by Hal Leonard Corporation. New releases of vocal folios for *A Little Princess* and Mr. Lippa's songbook are soon to follow. Mr. Lippa also contributed a choral piece to the *It Gets Better* campaign (premiered by musical theater students at Texas State University) which was released by Hal Leonard for middle and high school choruses in 2013.

Awards include a Tony® nomination, GRAMMY nomination, the Gilman/Gonzalez-Falla Theater Foundation Award, ASCAP's Richard Rodgers/New Horizons Award, The Drama Desk, The Outer Critics Circle and second place for the Alice B. Deucey Award for all- around outstanding fifth-grader (lost to Cynthia Fink). Memberships include ASCAP, Actors' Equity, the AF of M and The Dramatists Guild, where Mr. Lippa serves as Council member.

A graduate and supporter of the University of Michigan, Mr. Lippa was born in Leeds, England but grew up in suburban Detroit. He was ordained an Interfaith minister in 2013.
www.andrewlippa.com

BE THE HERO

Music and Lyrics by
ANDREW LIPPA

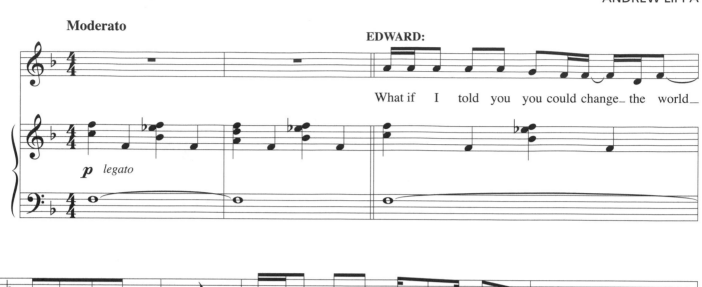

EDWARD:

What if I told you you could change the world with just one thought? What if I told you you could be a king?

An-y-thing you de-si - red boy, an-y-thing on a plate, all with-in your pow-er to cre-

ate. I know some-where in the dark - ness there's a sto-ry meant for me where I

-ro of your sto-ry, boy,_ and then you can rise__ to be__ the he-ro once_ a-gain.

What if I said I met a witch_ when I was ver-y young?_

What if I said she showed me how I die?__ Pow-er-less in the face_ of it,

35
ter-ri-fied in the wood, _ that was where my life was changed for good. Hey!

38
What if I said I met a gi - ant wast-ing in a cave?_ What if I claimed I rose to be___ far

41
brav-er than the brave?_ All___ my life of sto-ries, son,_ and ev-'ry-one___ is true,_

44
so be-lieve_ me as I'm tell-ing you___ to be the he-

tale that you in - vent_ can be__ a life that you__ make real,__ where each

char - ac - ter__ you meet_ be - comes_your friend._ You don't need to be__ a nov - el - ist to

make be - lieve_ what's wait - ing 'round the bend!_____ Be the he -

WOMEN:

Be the he -

MEN:

Be the he -

con - quer ev - 'ry chal-lenge, you can face each step-ping stone._ Be the he -

con - quer ev - 'ry chal-lenge, you can face each step-ping stone._ Be the he -

con - quer ev - 'ry chal-lenge, you can face each step-ping stone._ Be the he -

- ro of your sto - ry..._

- ro of your sto - ry..._

- ro of your sto - ry..._

What if I swore I saw a mer - maid swim-min' in__ the mist?

What if I told you she would be__ the first__ girl that I kissed?_ Out_

there in the wa - ter, filled with ea-ger-ness and fear,_ here is what she whis-pered in my

On a wing___ or on a prayer___ you get there

on - ly with__ your voice.__ Be at-ten - tive, be in-ven - tive, be the first__

(WOMEN):
Be at-ten - tive, be in-ven - tive, be the first__

(MEN):
Be at-ten - tive, be in-ven - tive, be the first__

one to re-joice. With a sto-ry in your heart you won't need

one to re-joice. With a sto-ry in your heart you won't need

one to re-joice. With a sto-ry in your heart you won't need

an - y oth-er choice. You're a he - ro, fight-ing drag-ons, win-ning

an - y oth-er choice. You're a he - ro, fight-ing drag-ons, win-ning

an - y oth-er choice. You're a he - ro, fight-ing drag-ons, win-ning

wars. Be the he-ro and the world will

wars. Be the he-ro and the world will

wars. Be the he-ro and the world will

soon be yours!

soon be yours!

soon be yours!

THE WITCH

Music and Lyrics by
ANDREW LIPPA

Funky "4", not fast

avoid sustain pedal as much as possible

WITCH:

What's your con-cern? Are you scared of hear-ing one thing new when you could learn some-thing se-cret that could

detached, not legato

help you through? In one good turn, I can show you coun-ter - feit from true. Life be - gins_

A little brighter

_ when you know_ how it ends._

WITCH: *And yours is no ordinary life.*

You've be - come im - por - tant; you're_ the brav - est man a - round._

You're the kind_ with vir - tue, al - ways find - ing com-mon ground.__ You

climb each hill in front of you,_ with - out a suf-ferin' sound,_ com -

Don't be - lieve the fair - y tales_ that say life is a breeze. __

Ev - 'ry man must face a trial_ that brings him to his knees. __ But

let me share a mag - ic truth,_ a proof of all__ that thrives. __ The

may be dis-ap-point - ed, but you may be ov-er-joyed!

ooh!

ALL WITCHES:

So,_____ don't be sad, don't be scared, be al - ert,

sfz *p* *sub.*

crescendo poco a poco

be pre-pared, take a breath, take it slow, let un-cer - tain-ty go,___ when you know___

STRANGER

Music and Lyrics by
ANDREW LIPPA

TWO MEN IN MY LIFE

Music and Lyrics by
ANDREW LIPPA

SANDRA:

OUT THERE ON THE ROAD

Music and Lyrics by
ANDREW LIPPA

Funky Country

You can take a jour - ney through this coun - try's flesh and blood.

On a ride past count - ry side and Mis - sis - sip - pi mud.

Hit the street with two big feet to bear your heav - y load and

live life out there on the road.

An - y - one_ you wan - na be_ and an - y - thing_ you say,_

come to - mor - row you'll_ be free_ of who you are to - day._

Ac - tion and ad - ven - ture when you change your fixed a - bode._ Go

live life out there on the road._ Would-n't you

One big pair of shoes!_____ We were born to wake_ each morn' some

place we've nev-er been.__ Check-in' out__ the lo-cals as they

watch us check-in' in.__ Ev-'ry new en-coun-ter in an-

oth-er new_ zip code,_ we'll find it out there....__

Funky feel again
43
EDWARD:
Wait! He's not a mon - ster. He's a think - er, he's a whiz!
WOMEN:
ff
That's him right there!
MEN:
ff
That's him right there!
ff
8vb
46
This boy is - n't half as bad as you all think he is.
(8vb)
48
+KARL 8vb
I've been so in - spir - ed, I've de - cid - ed we're a pair.
We're head - ing out there on the road!
(8vb)

L'stesso tempo

JENNY:
Ed - ward Bloom, don't tell me that_ you're leav - ing us for good._

EDWARD:
Jen-ny, yes I'm leav-ing, but_ "for good"_ I nev-er could. _ I'll be back_ some-day._

JENNY:
And I'll_ be

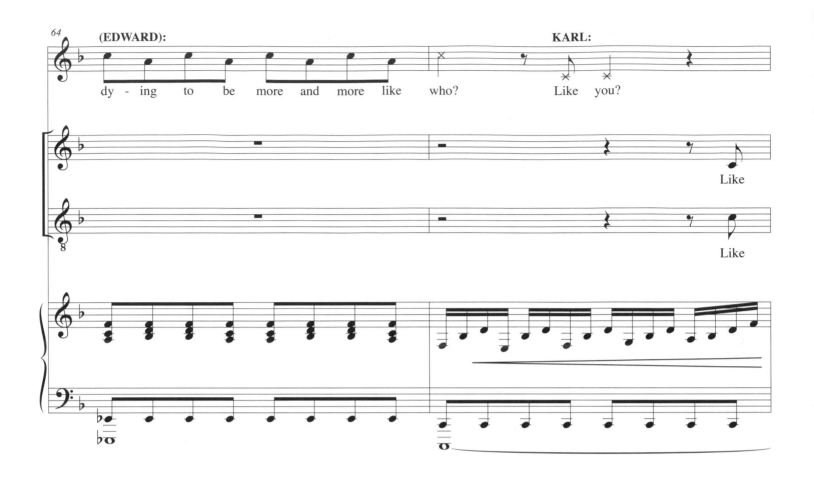

TIME STOPS

Music and Lyrics by
ANDREW LIPPA

still, your heart is beat - ing. Time stops, though you don't take a breath.

She's there___ and all you've___ ev - er want - ed is near - er,___

clear - er._____ I used to think___ the world___ was small.

Now I don't think that way at all.___ Time stops, when

dreams come true be-fore you. Time stops, when fan-tas-y___ is real.___

I knew___ this mo-ment was ex-pect-ed. But this good?_____

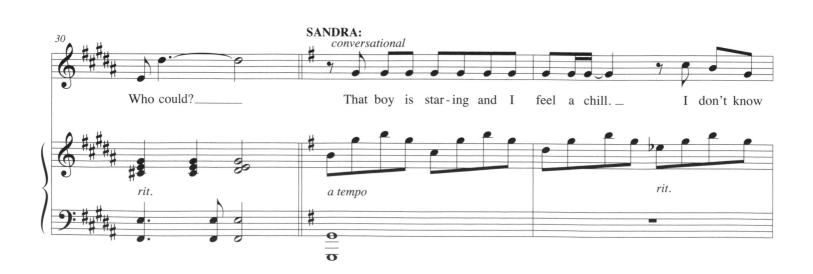

SANDRA:
conversational

Who could?_____ That boy is star-ing and I feel a chill. ___ I don't know

Time stops,_ and trou-bles_ are a-ban-doned. Time stops,_ the

more! And trou-bles_ are a-ban-doned. Time stops,_ the

a tempo

min-ute_ she ar-rives. I've seen_ the fu-ture in this in-stant, sub-

min-ute_ he ar-rives. I've seen_ the fu-ture in this in-stant, sub-

ver - sive,_____ sub - lime!

ver - sive,_____ sub - lime!

DAFFODILS

Music and Lyrics by
ANDREW LIPPA

Strong, confident

EDWARD:

I was in-den-tured to a trav-'ling cir - cus,

el - e - phants and all.___ I was shot out of a can-non when they

up and lost__ the ball.___ I met were-wolves, gi-ants, danc-ing bears. If

you don't think__ it true,___ then how on Earth can you ex-plain__ the road__ that

sim.

breeze.

Driving but not faster

And like that mom-ent right be - tween a-sleep and wak-ing, I thought I saw ten thou-sand

strong in one quick_ glance. _ But when I saw your face, I knew be-yond mis-tak-ing, a

rit.

mil - lion flow-ers could-n't stand_ a chance. So I'll pre-tend the

mf

rit.

daf - fo-dils are just an in - tro-duc-tion to the blos-som-ing of me and you. Be-side the lake, be-neath the tree, be-yond mis-take. Please mar - ry me. Please mar - ry me.

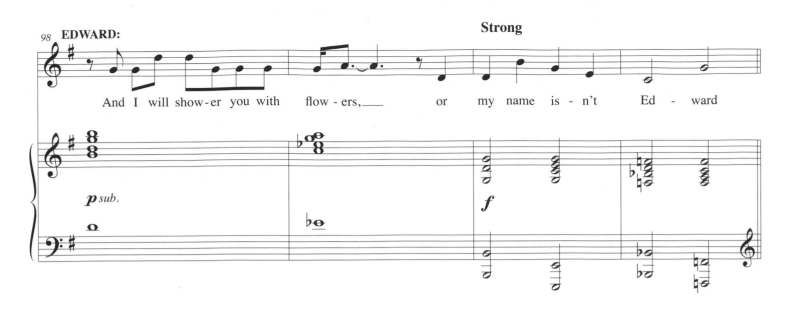

And I will show-er you with flow-ers,___ or my name is-n't Ed - ward

Bloom.___

FIGHT THE DRAGONS

Music and Lyrics by
ANDREW LIPPA

stay-in' still— is play-in' dead,— the kind who's look-in' for - ward to____ the

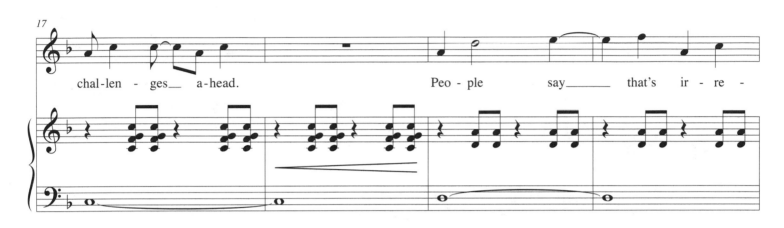

chal-len - ges__ a-head. Peo - ple say____ that's ir - re -

spon - si - ble.__ Peo - ple tell____ me, "Stay at

home." But I'm not__ made____ for things like

mow-in' lawns___ or a - pron strings.___ I'm___ my___ best_____ when

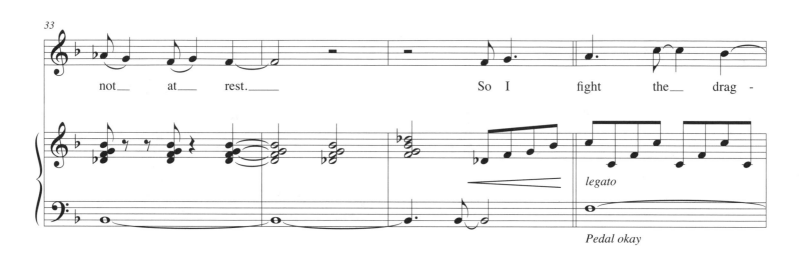

not___ at___ rest._____ So I fight the___ drag -

legato

Pedal okay

- ons and I storm the___ cas - tles and I win a___ bat -

- tle or___ two._____ Then comes the day_____ it's___ time___

like fif - ty thou - sand_ drums____ all bang - ing, bring my___ sto -

ries home_ to you. And I won - der as I wan-

-der on the road_ from door to door,_ ex - act - ly what you think_

___ of where I've been.___ Do you know___ I joined the cir-

you'll come to me__ one day__

and say: Let's fight the__ drag-ons__ and then storm the__ cas-tles, 'til we

No pedal

win what__ needs__ to be__ won.__ So when I'm old__

__ and__ tired__ you'll do the job__ re - quired.__ You'll be__ there

boy in - to_____ a big - ger man.

So I'll fight the_ drag -

rit.

ons_____ 'til_ you can._____

rit.

I DON'T NEED A ROOF

Music and Lyrics by
ANDREW LIPPA

I don't need a roof to say I'm cov-ered.

I don't need a roof to know I'm home.

There could be a sin-gle shin-gle dan-gling o-ver-head.

I don't need a roof to make my

knows: Af - ter__ the rain, some - thing grows.

I don't need_ a roof_ to say_ I love you.

I don't need_ a roof__ to call_ you mine.

I don't need ad - ven - ture in some far a - way_ fron - tier._

I don't need_ a roof_ to feel_ you

near. All I need_ is you,_ and you_ for - ev - er.

All I feel_ is true_ and ab - so - lute.

I don't need a le - gal deed to help me_ play my

WHAT'S NEXT

Music and Lyrics by
ANDREW LIPPA

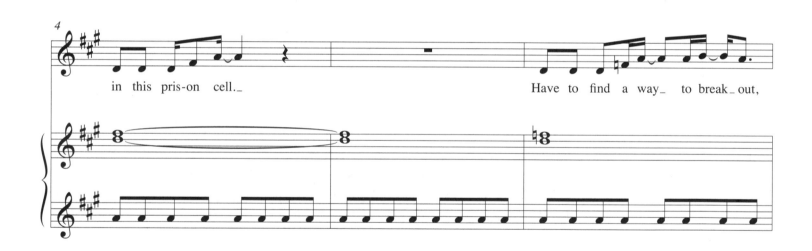

step out of ___ your state ___ of shock, ___ we on - ly need ___ to pick ___ this lock. ___

"What's next?" is all an - y - one

needs to be - gin. "What's next?" has been a

friend to you. ___ What's next to do? ___ One word and then sud - den - ly one more a - gain.

mf

sim.

Only one dad on - ly in - spir - ing one son.

Ed - ward, you're done writ - ing your per - fect tale, tell - ing the

per - fect tale. It was a per - fect

tale.

mp cresc. poco a poco

rit.

HOW IT ENDS

Music and Lyrics by
ANDREW LIPPA

THIS RIVER BETWEEN US

Music and Lyrics by
ANDREW LIPPA

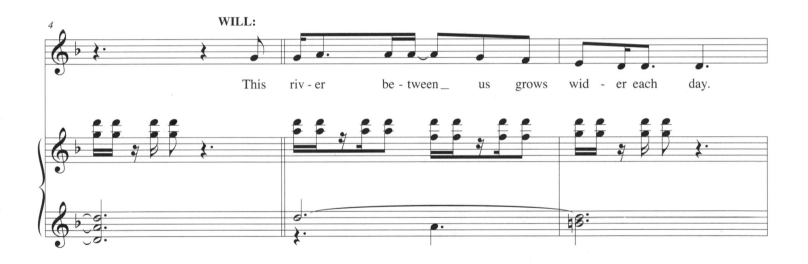

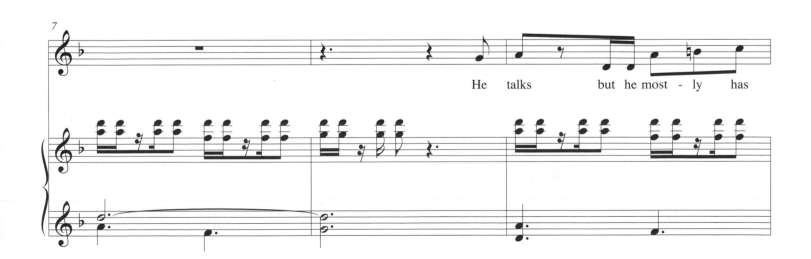

soon as he'll start, but his fan - cy ex - cites him so Ed - ward takes

heart._____ He prom - ised he'd re -

strain him - self.___ He prom - ised he'd be good. He

prom - ised he'd con - tain him - self, as if he ev - er

could._____ My fa - ther speaks and shoot-ing stars___ can

f molto agitato

No pedal

fill the skies a - bove you._____ So why don't I be -

Pedal

lieve my fath - er when he says, "I love you?"_____

f

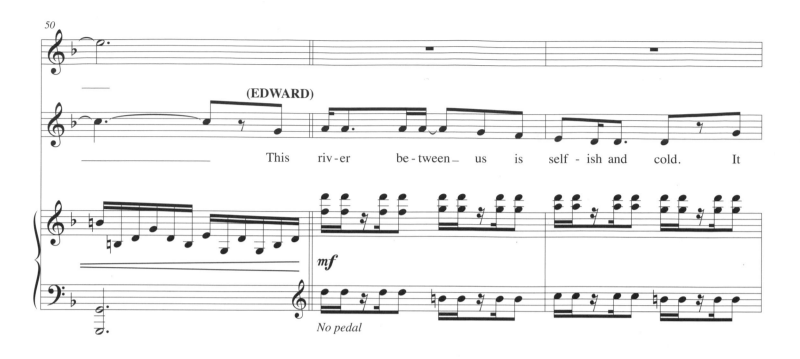

(EDWARD)

This riv-er be-tween_ us is self-ish and cold. It

flows where it wants to, it can't be con-trolled. My son does-n't want me to be_

_ what I am. He don't give a damn!_

A STORY OF MY OWN

Music and Lyrics by
ANDREW LIPPA

shore, the dip-lo-mat-ic corps, and ev-er-more a

sto-ry of my own! Say I'm head-ed for glo-ry, say I'm head-ed for

Pedal okay

jail. Say the words that e-rase an-y trace of this place and each

rec-og-nized face on this been-there-and-done-that trail!___ They'll hear a sto-ry of my

Moun-tains sun-ny and feared un - cross - a - ble. Pyr - a-mids and gi - ant squids and

chick-en cor-don bleu! Ac-com-plish-ments ga - lore, a per-fect bowl-ing

score. I'd just a-dore a sto - ry of my

own! Send me off to the gal - lows, send me off to the slum. My di-

Pedal okay

rec-tion is clear, an-y set-ting but here, let my fu-ture ap-pear, show me some-one who I can be-

come! So throw me a crumb that's from a sto-ry of my

own, with pow-er to a-muse. And ev-'ry line with-

As little pedal as possible

in its spine, in prose di-vine, u-nan-i-mous re-views! The un-ex-pect-ed

STRANGER

Music and Lyrics by
ANDREW LIPPA

wish I knew the man,_____ but he's a

strang - er._ My fa - ther is__ a strang - er I__ know

ver - y well._ A puz - zling shell.

Hope - ful._ What's on its way_ may help us both to grow,_

try, I'll real-ly try. And in time my boy is sure to see_

molto rit. *colla voce*

bright-er days_ for Dad and me. We can do_ things bet-ter than be - fore. So that

rit.

strang - ers we will be_____ no

a tempo

more._____

f *a tempo* *rit.*